TALES FROM AMERICANA

The Jersey Devil

BY MARLEY RICHMOND

Kids Core
An Imprint of Abdo Publishing
abdobooks.com

abdobooks.com

Published by Abdo Publishing, a division of ABDO, PO Box 398166, Minneapolis, Minnesota 55439.

Printed in the United States of America, North Mankato, Minnesota.
102023
012024

THIS BOOK CONTAINS RECYCLED MATERIALS

Cover Photo: Daniel Eskridge/Shutterstock Images
Interior Photos: Sudarat Lofqvist/Shutterstock Images, 4–5; Library of Congress, 6, 28 (bottom); Chronicle/Alamy, 8, 28 (top); Luciana Serra/Shutterstock Images, 10–11; Paolo Bona/Shutterstock Images, 13; Shutterstock Images, 14, 25; Red Line Editorial, 16; Montri Thipsorn/Shutterstock Images, 18, 29 (top); Mike Stobe/NHLI/Getty Images, 20–21; Bettmann/Getty Images, 22; RGR Collection/Alamy, 24, 29 (bottom); Matthew Corrigan/Alamy, 26

Editor: Angela Lim
Series Designer: Katharine Hale

Library of Congress Control Number: 2023939742

Publisher's Cataloging-in-Publication Data

Names: Richmond, Marley, author.
Title: The Jersey Devil / by Marley Richmond
Description: Minneapolis, Minnesota: Abdo Publishing, 2024 | Series: Tales from Americana | Includes online resources and index.
Identifiers: ISBN 9781098292843 (lib. bdg.) | ISBN 9798384910787 (ebook)
Subjects: LCSH: Jersey Devil (Monster)--Juvenile literature. | New Jersey--Pine Barrens--Juvenile literature. | Animals, Mythical--Juvenile literature. | Folklore--Juvenile literature. | Cryptozoology--Juvenile literature.
Classification: DDC 398.24--dc23

CONTENTS

Stories say the Jersey Devil was born on a dark, stormy night.

CHAPTER 1

Birth of the Jersey Devil

It was 1735. Wind howled in the forest. Lightning flashed across the night sky. There was a small house near the trees. Its windows glowed with candlelight. Mother Leeds was giving birth inside. This would be her thirteenth child.

According to legends, the Leeds House is the birthplace of the Jersey Devil.

Mother Leeds had little money. She lived in a small town. It is now called Leeds Point, New Jersey. Mother Leeds's home was near the Pine Barrens. This area was known for its spooky forests. Mist gathered among the trees.

Sometimes, the streams in the Pine Barrens looked as if they were full of red water.

The forest became even scarier after Mother Leeds's baby was born. The baby looked healthy at first. But soon he began to change. First, he grew a long tail. Then wings popped out from his back. His hands became claws.

Advances in Medicine

In the 1700s, medical knowledge was not as good as it is today. Historians think that Mother Leeds's baby may have been born with a **birth defect**. In the past, many people wrongly believed that a birth defect was a sign of evil. Scientists now know more about the real causes of birth defects, such as the mother being very sick while pregnant.

The Jersey Devil looks like a mixture of many animals.

His feet became hooves. The creature flew out the window into the stormy night. The baby became the Jersey Devil.

A New Jersey Legend

The story of the Jersey Devil is a **legend**. The creature is also called the Leeds Devil. People have told tales about this creature for hundreds of years.

The Jersey Devil is said to have long legs and short arms. It has a bat's wings, a tail, and glowing red eyes. Its screech can be heard across the forest. Some stories say the creature has the head of a horse. Others say it has the head and horns of a goat. Some people claim to have seen this creature. But few people truly believe that it exists.

Explore Online

Visit the website below. Does it give any new information about the Pine Barrens that wasn't in Chapter One?

The Jersey Devil and Folklore

abdocorelibrary.com/jersey-devil

People sometimes share scary stories around a campfire.

CHAPTER 2

A Creature in the Woods

Legends of the Jersey Devil were passed down as **oral** tales for many years. The first written story about the Jersey Devil was published in the *Atlantic Monthly* in 1959. It told the story of Mother Leeds and the Jersey Devil's birth.

But there are other explanations for how the legend began. Mother Leeds was married to Daniel Leeds. He wrote and published books. Some people did not like what Daniel Leeds wrote.

A few people published bad things about Daniel Leeds. They called him the devil. The Leeds family **crest** showed three creatures with bat wings and scary faces. Some people said these creatures were devils. They spread rumors

Animal Explanations

Some people think the Jersey Devil is actually a hammer-headed bat. This creature has a horselike head. Its wings stretch 3 feet (1 m) wide. It looks like the legendary Jersey Devil. But it lives in Africa, not North America.

A family crest is a symbol that represents the history of a family.

about the Leeds family and their crest. These rumors may have turned into stories about the Jersey Devil.

Sightings of the Jersey Devil have been reported across New Jersey.

Legends are sometimes used to explain bad things that have no clear cause.

Famous Sightings

Sightings of the Jersey Devil have been reported since the 1700s. Some of the most famous reports came in 1909. There were more than 30 sightings in one week. Reports came from New Jersey, Maryland, Pennsylvania, and Delaware.

Some people claimed they saw the creature. Others said they saw its tracks. One local saw hoofprints in the snow. They were made by a two-legged animal. These reports matched the legends about the Jersey Devil's appearance.

The Jersey Devil is said to have hooves and walk on two legs.

Reports of the Jersey Devil continued. In 1960, a zoo in New Jersey offered a $10,000 reward to whomever could catch the creature. But no one ever did.

Primary Source

Some people have reported signs of the Jersey Devil. Grace-Ellen McCrann described one of these reports from 1909. She wrote:

> Councilman E. P. Weeden . . . claimed to have been awoken by flapping wings. . . . [He] said he found **cloven** footprints in the snow.

Source: Grace-Ellen McCrann. "Legend of the New Jersey Devil." *New Jersey Historical Society*, 26 Oct. 2000, jerseyhistory.org. Accessed 4 May 2023.

What's the Big Idea?

Read this quote carefully. What is its main idea? Explain how the main idea is supported by details.

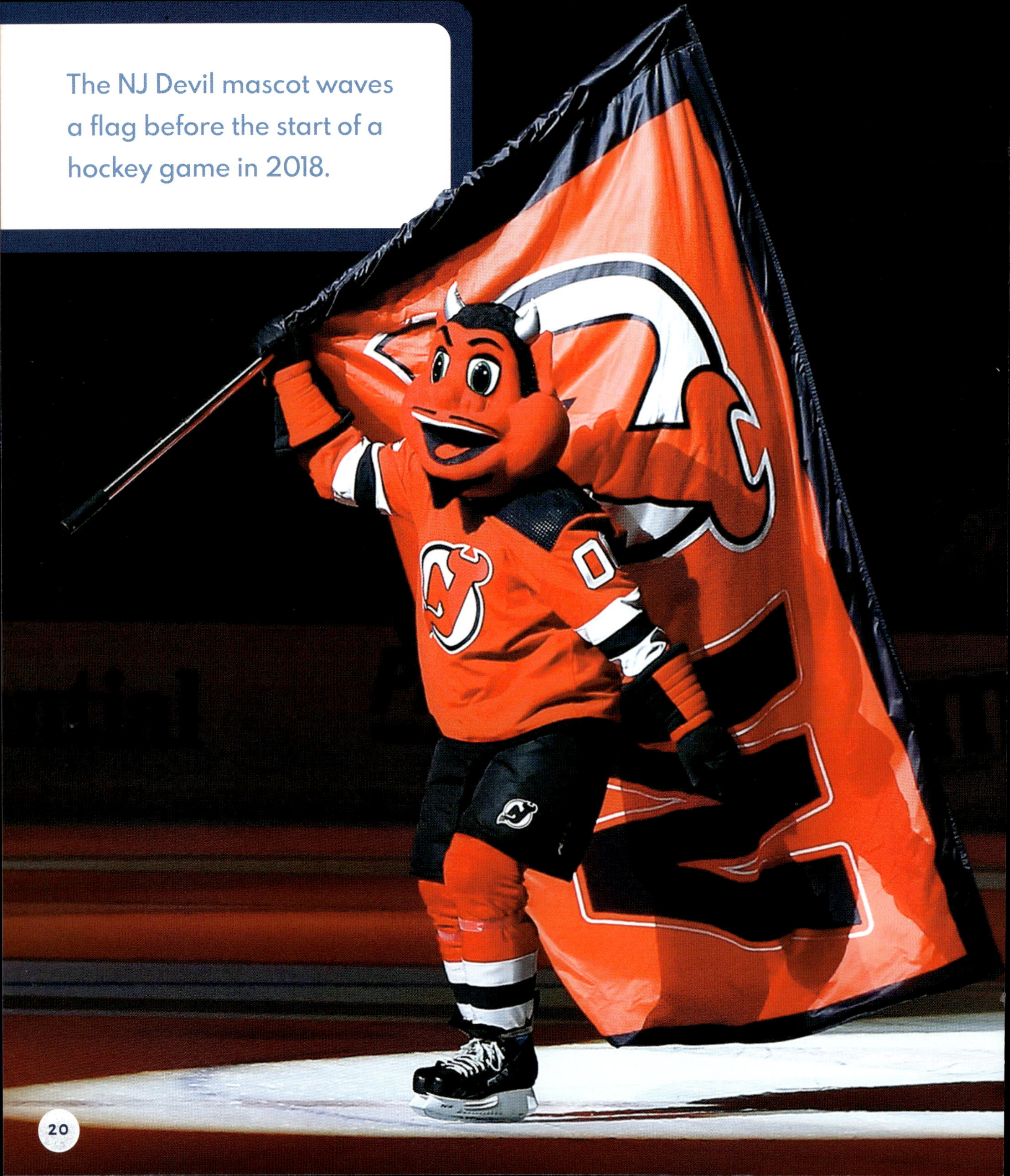

The NJ Devil mascot waves a flag before the start of a hockey game in 2018.

CHAPTER 3

The Jersey Devil Today

The Jersey Devil remains a popular story in New Jersey. The state's National Hockey League team is named after the legend. But its mascot does not have a horse's head or bat's wings.

The Jersey Devil is an American legend.

The episode is an example of how legends can change over time.

Legends about the Jersey Devil have been passed down for hundreds of years. These stories may scare locals or explain hard times. They still have a place in culture today. People visiting the Pine Barrens may even believe they hear the sound of the Jersey Devil's shrieks.

Further Evidence

Look at the website below. Does it give any new evidence to support Chapter Three?

New Jersey Devil

abdocorelibrary.com/jersey-devil

Legendary Facts

The Jersey Devil has bat's wings, a tail, and the head of a goat or horse.

The Jersey Devil is said to have been born in the Leeds House in the New Jersey Pine Barrens.

People have reported seeing the Jersey Devil and its hoofprints.

The Jersey Devil has appeared in movies and pop culture.

Index

About the Author

Marley Richmond is a children's book editor and author. She lives in Minnesota with her cat, Bean.